Computer and Applications

Fundamentals

Coloring Book For Kids & Adults

Learning & Reward Coloring Pages

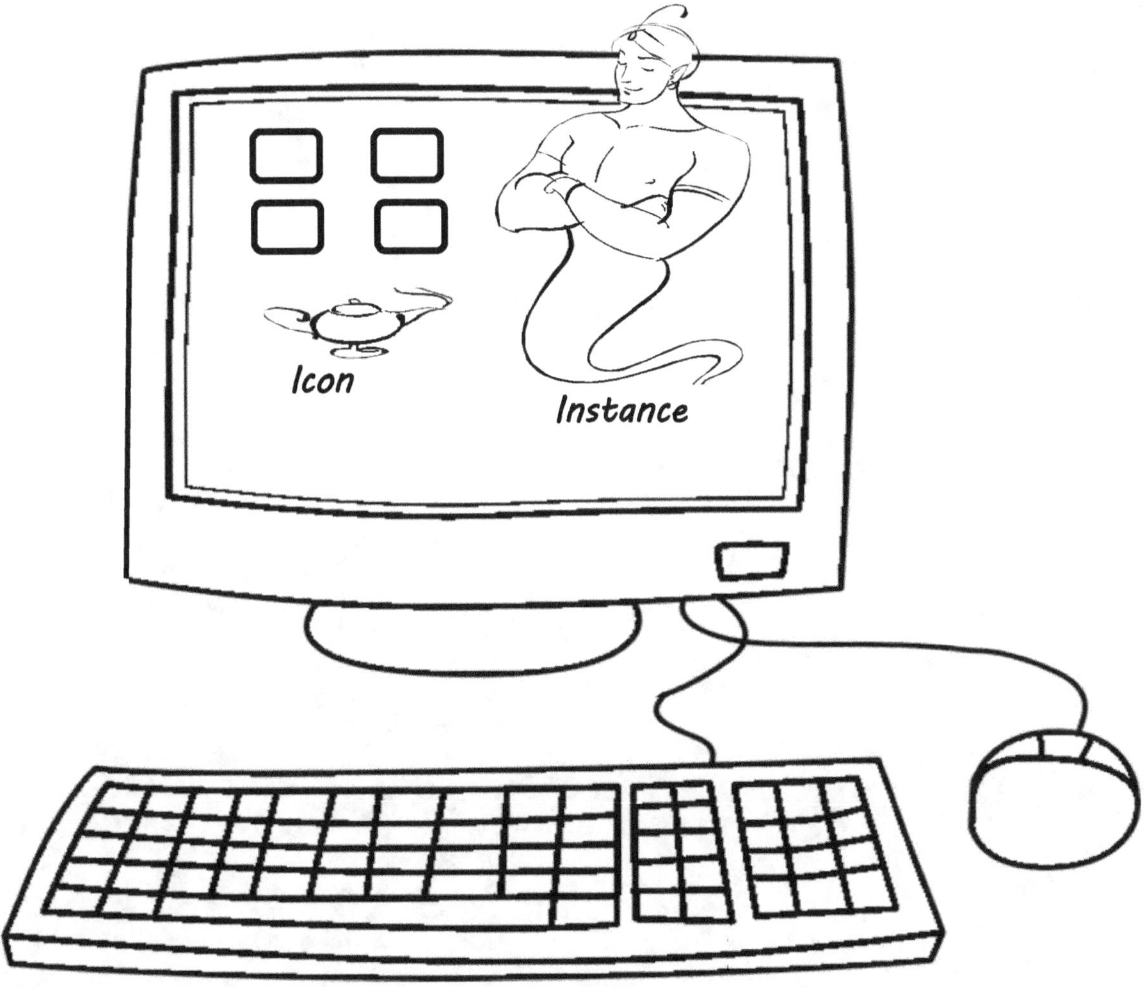

Icon

Instance

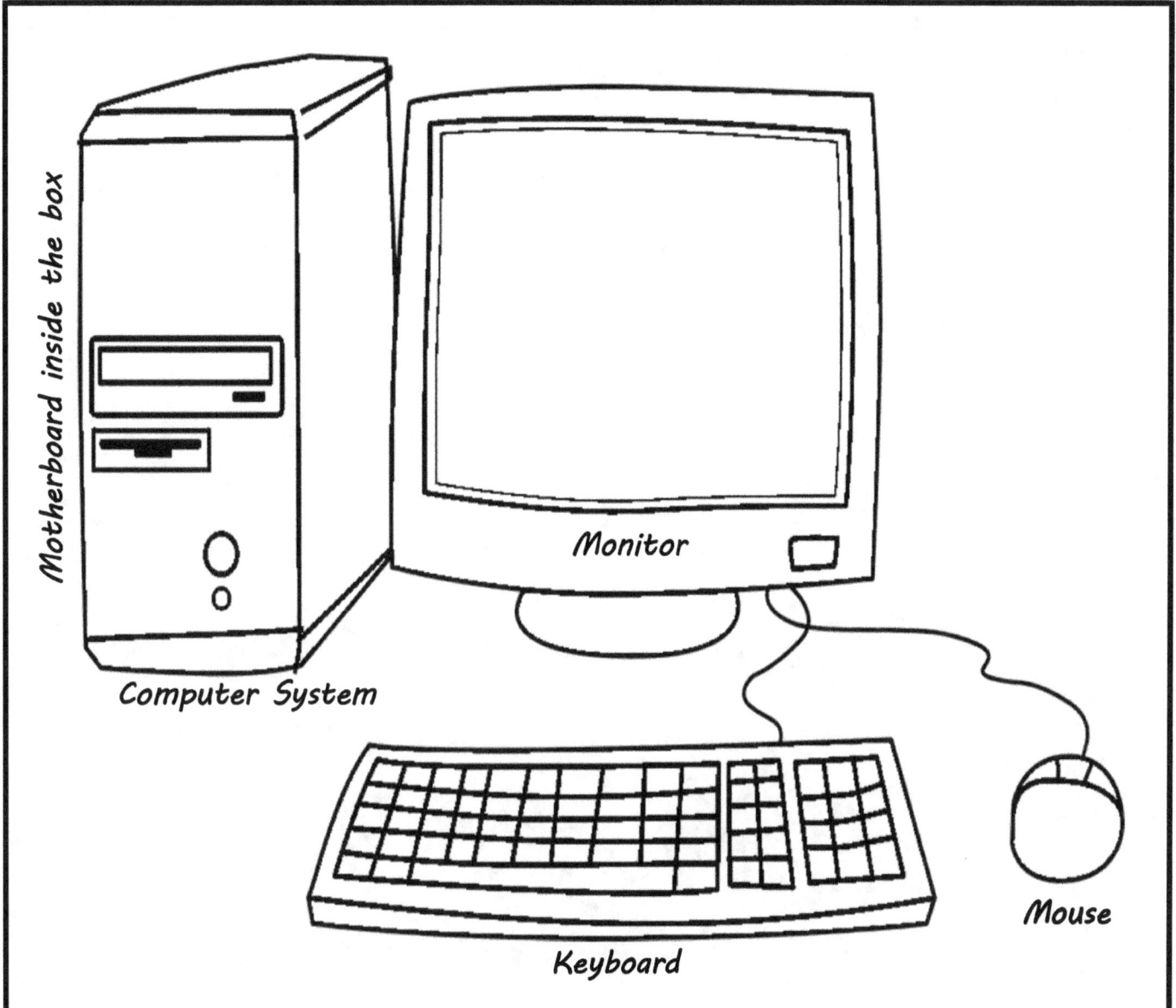

Computer System

Motherboard inside the box

Monitor

Keyboard

Mouse

Desktop Computer & Main parts

<u>Mouse</u> is used to move the pointer on the monitor and click.
<u>Keyboard</u> is for entering information. <u>Computer System Unit</u> is
an enclosure where motherboard resides. <u>Motherboard</u> is where
the microprocessor and other electronic components are. <u>Monitor</u> is where the output from microprocessor is displayed.

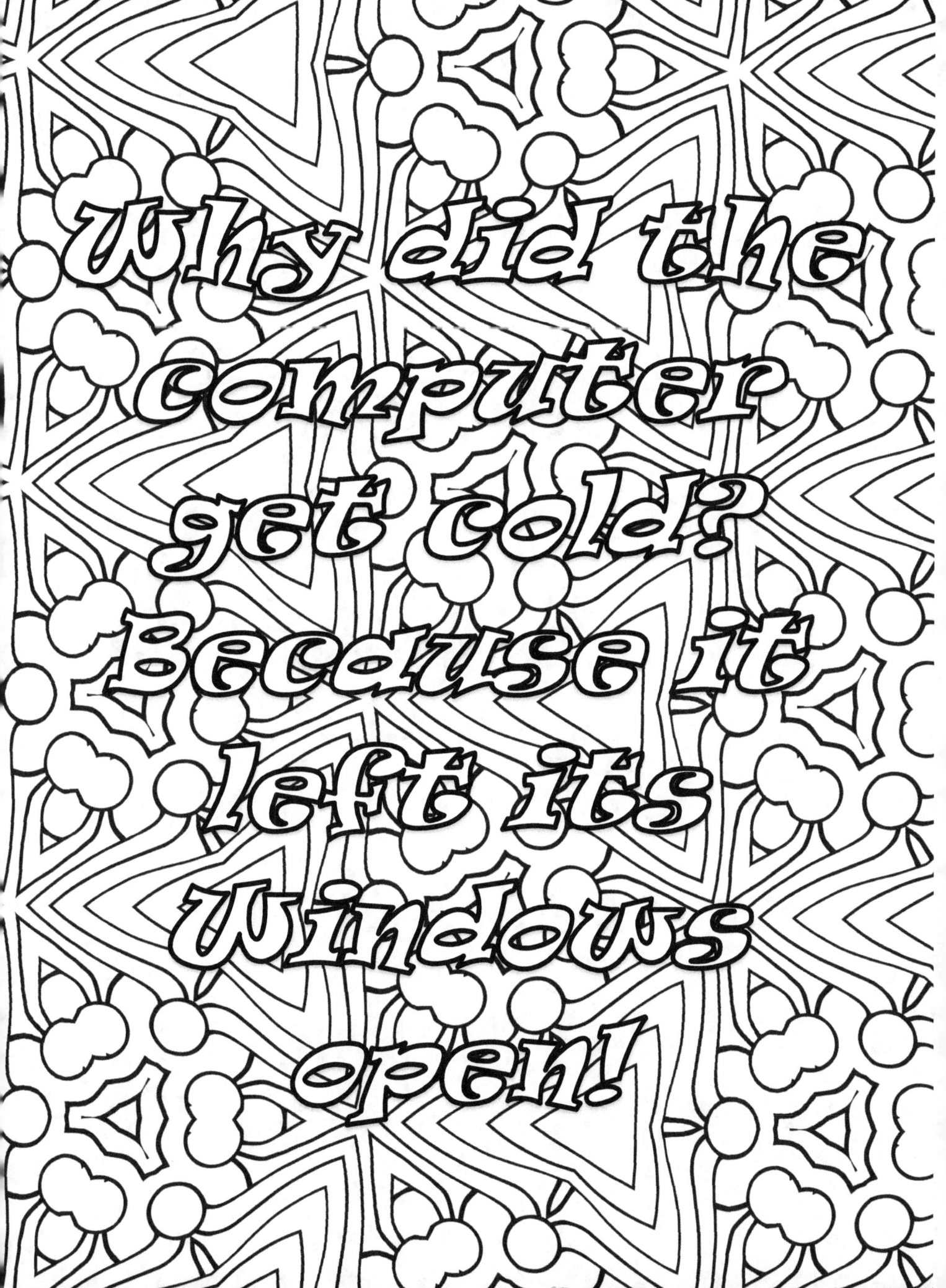

Why did the computer get cold? Because it left its Windows open!

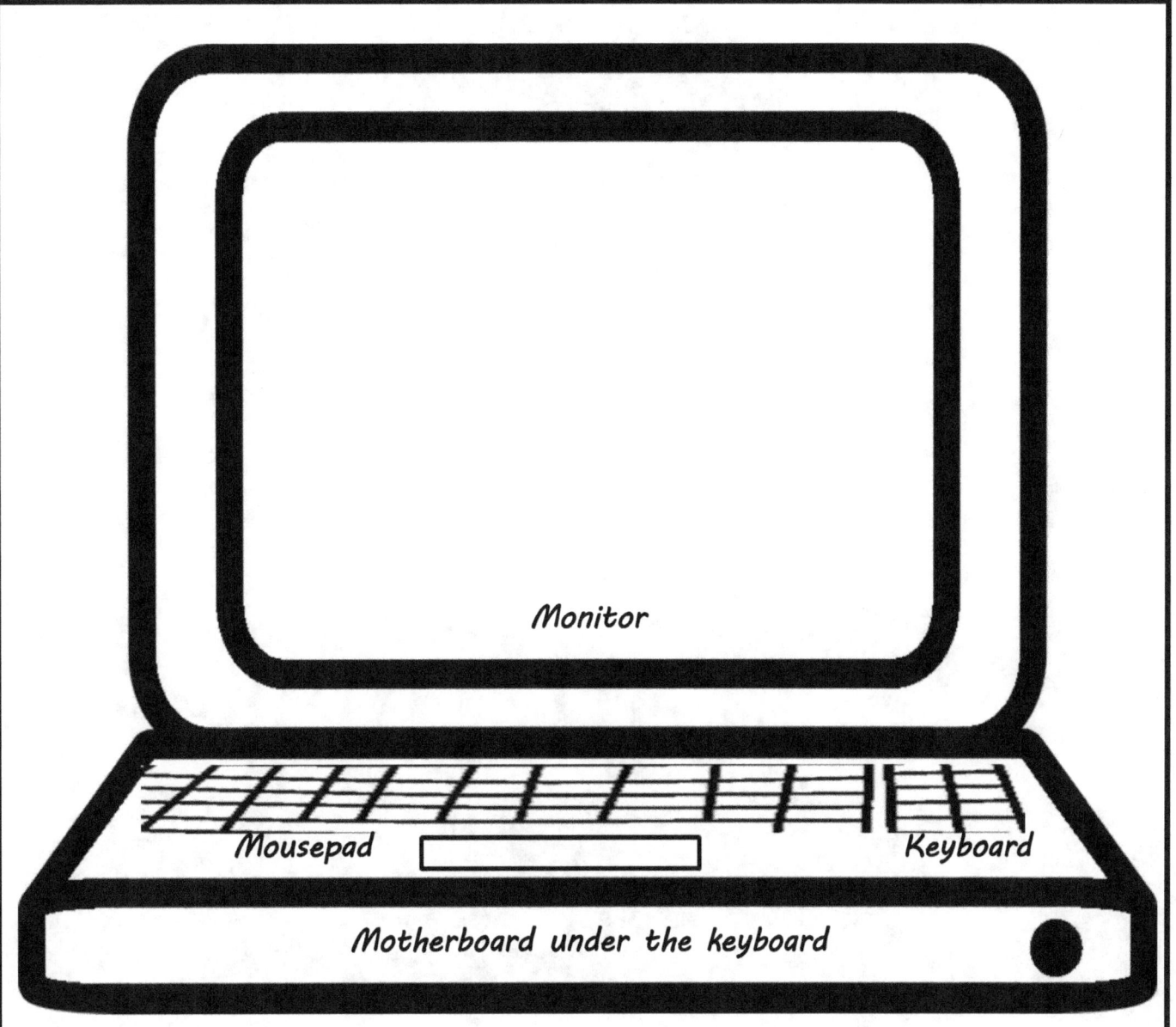

Laptop Computer & Main parts

Mousepad is used to move the pointer on the monitor and click. _Keyboard_ is for entering information. _Motherboard_ is where the microprocessor and other electronic components are and it's under the keyboard. _Monitor_ is where the output from microprocessor is displayed.

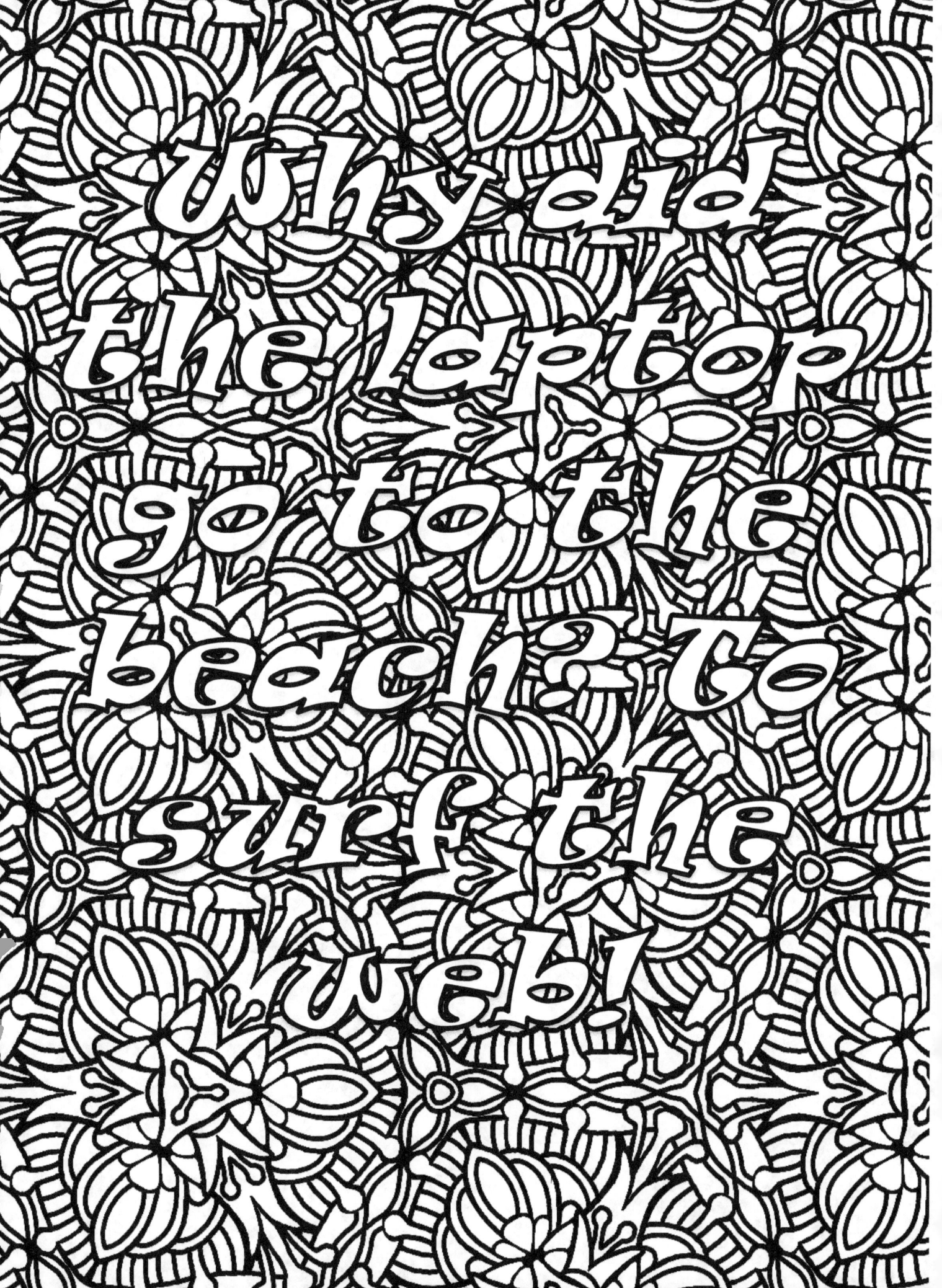

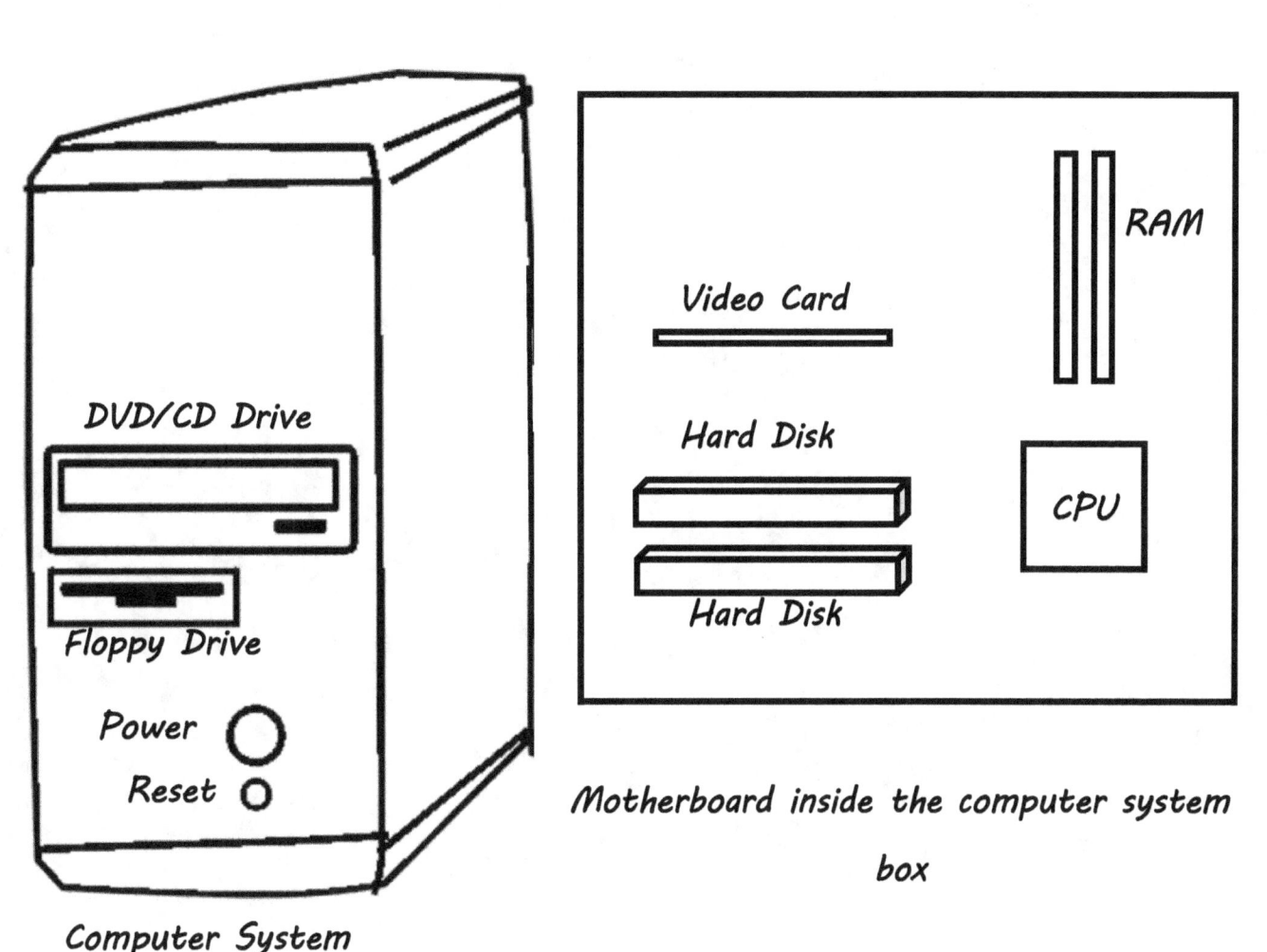

DVD/CD Drive

Floppy Drive

Power

Reset

Computer System

Video Card

Hard Disk

Hard Disk

RAM

CPU

Motherboard inside the computer system box

Motherboard and its Main Components

CPU (central processing unit aka microprocessor) is the brain of the computer and usually the fastest electronic component. Hard Disk is where the information is saved permanently. Hard disks cannot keep up with speed of CPU therefore RAM (random access memory aka not permanent) is used. Cable from video card connects to the monitor.

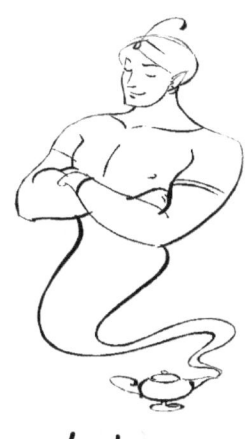
Instance

How many instances of Microsoft Word does it take to change a lightbulb? None, it's not a feature in the soft- ware!

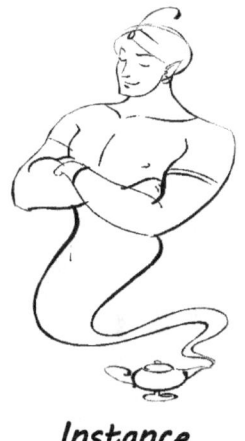
Instance

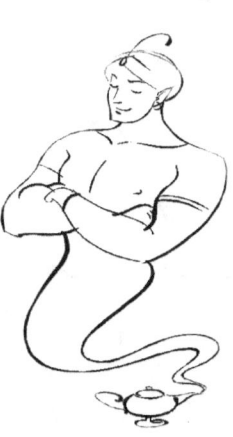
Instance

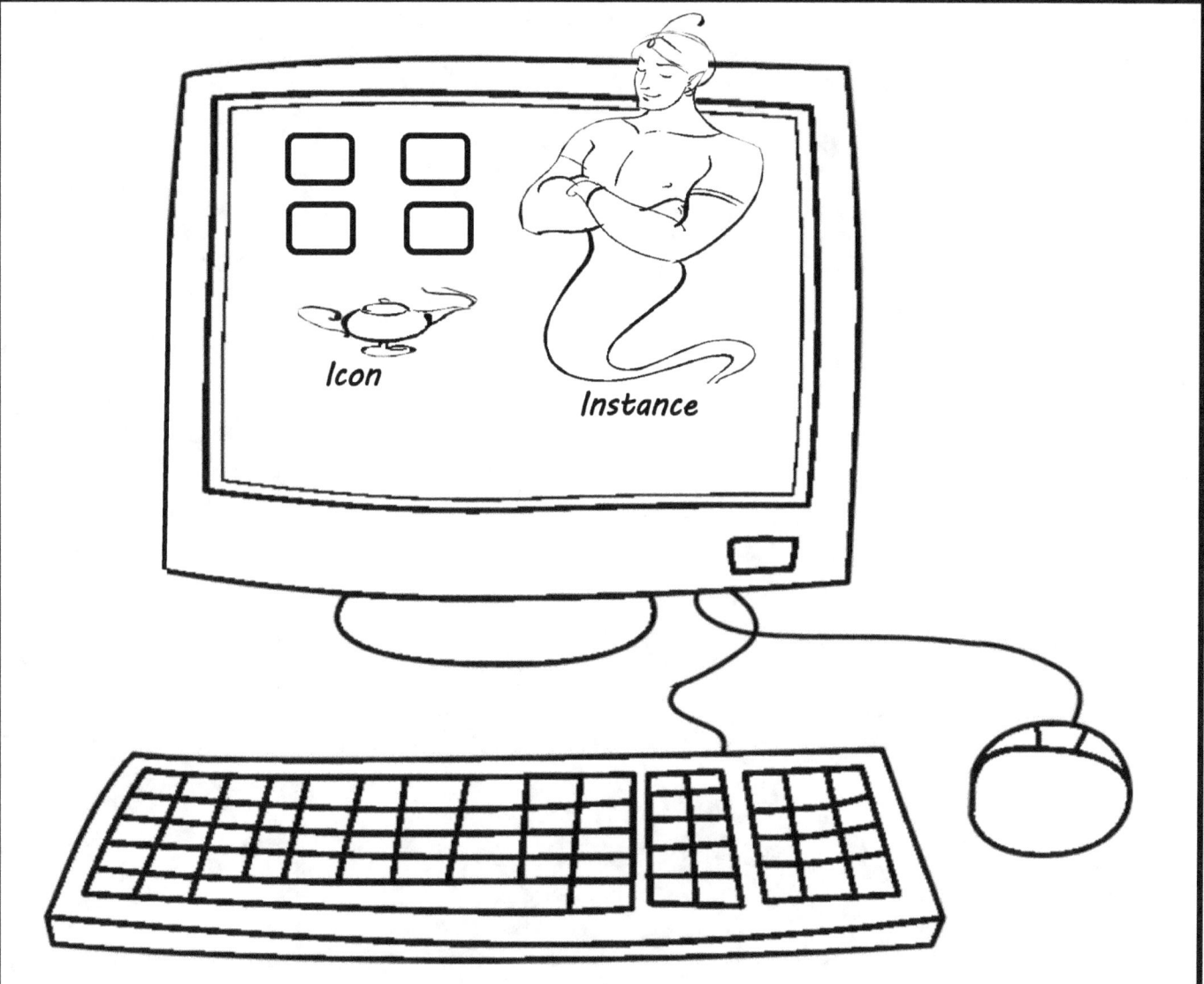

Icon

Instance

Beautiful icons on Screen (aka Desktop)

When you power ON the computer system, your computer screen will be having several small pictures, usually square in shape. Those are called icons. The whole screen is called Desktop. Each icon is clickable represent the application installed on your computer. Double clicking the icon will result in application becoming an instance. Without turning an installed application into an instance, the application remains useless. We interact with instance of an application to accomplish task.

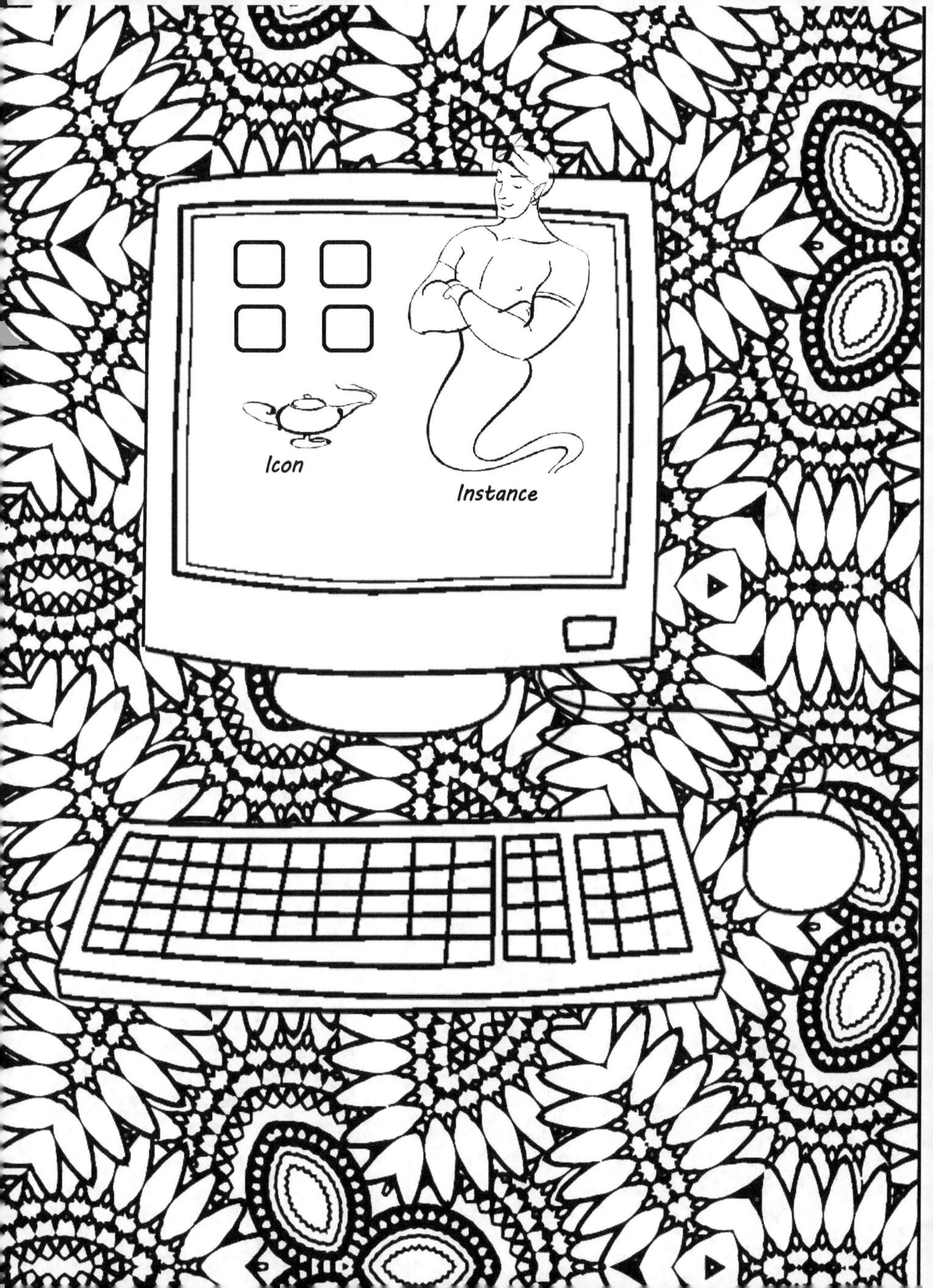

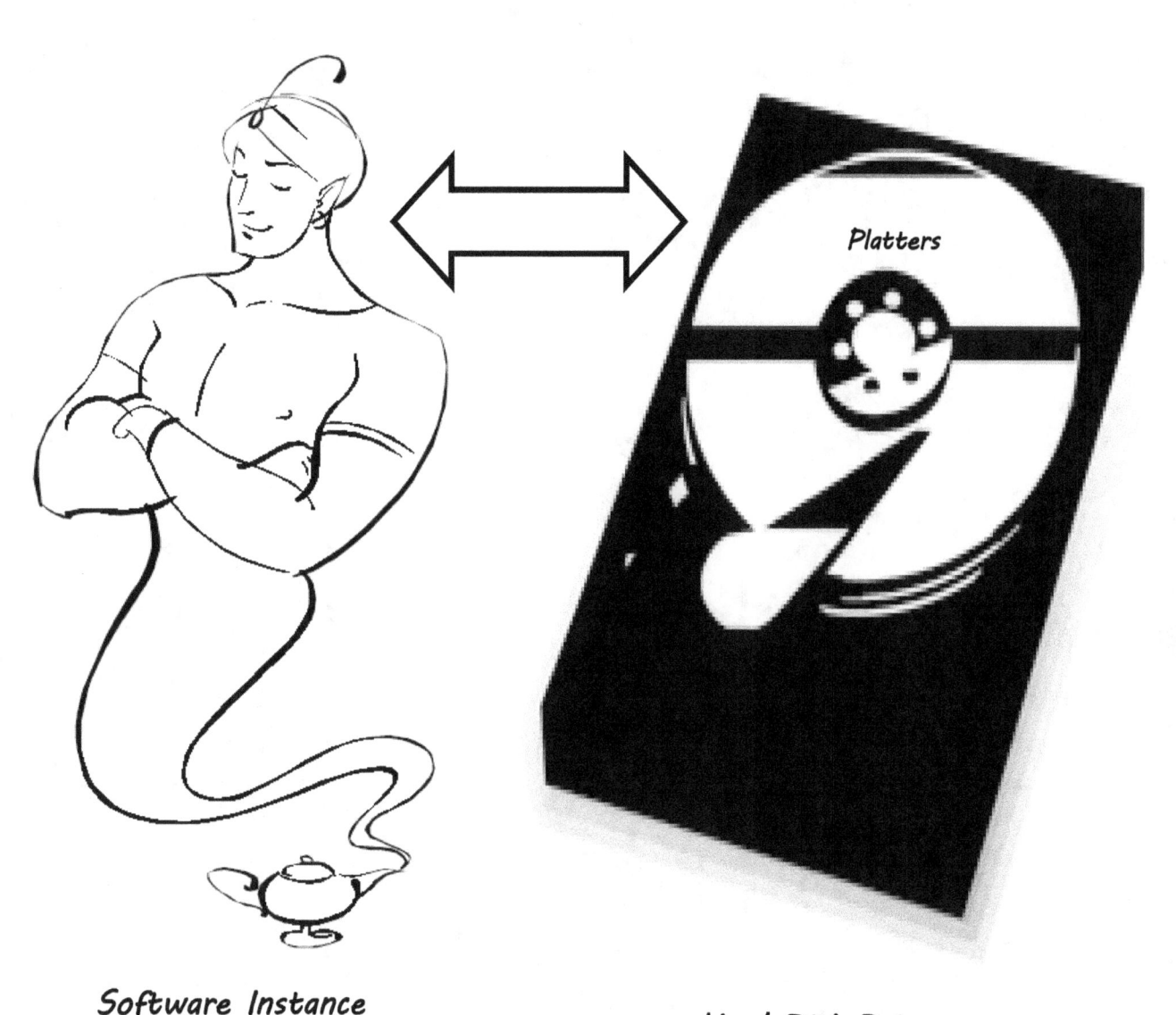

Software Instance

Platters

Hard Disk Drive

Data on Hard Disk Drive

There is only one way to save the data on Hard Disk Drive (HDD) i.e. in the form of files. These files are saved on platters (circular disks that spin) using the Actuator Arms and on request of software instance.

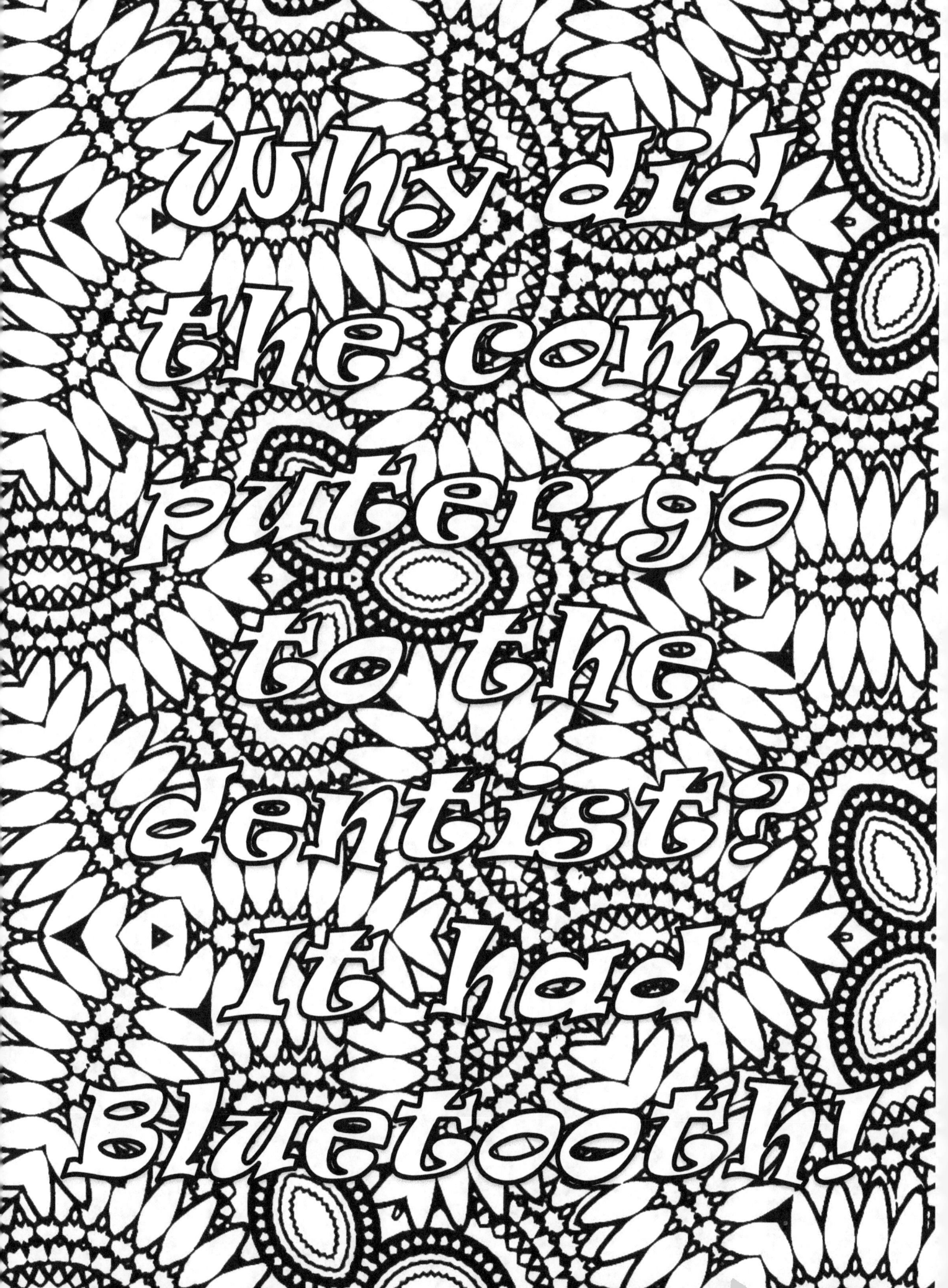

Why did the computer go to the dentist? It had Bluetooth!

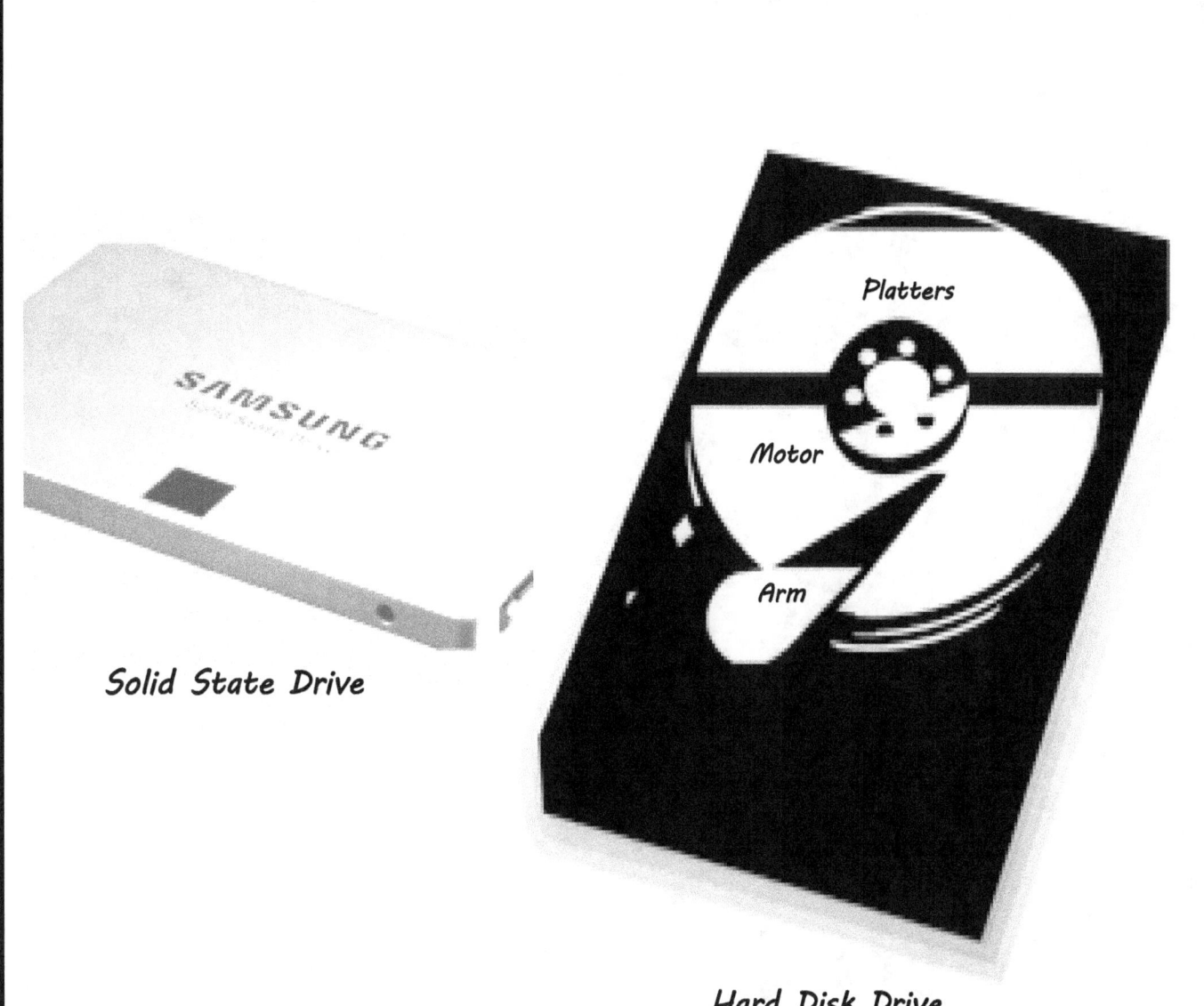

Solid State Drive

Hard Disk Drive

Solid State Drives

Solid State Drives (SSD) are comparatively newer storage devices and in them there is no arm that writes data on the rotating platters. There is no motor or any moving parts. Usually SSDs are better than Hard Disk Drive (HDD).

Why did the hard disk refuse to go to the gym? It didn't want to become a solid state

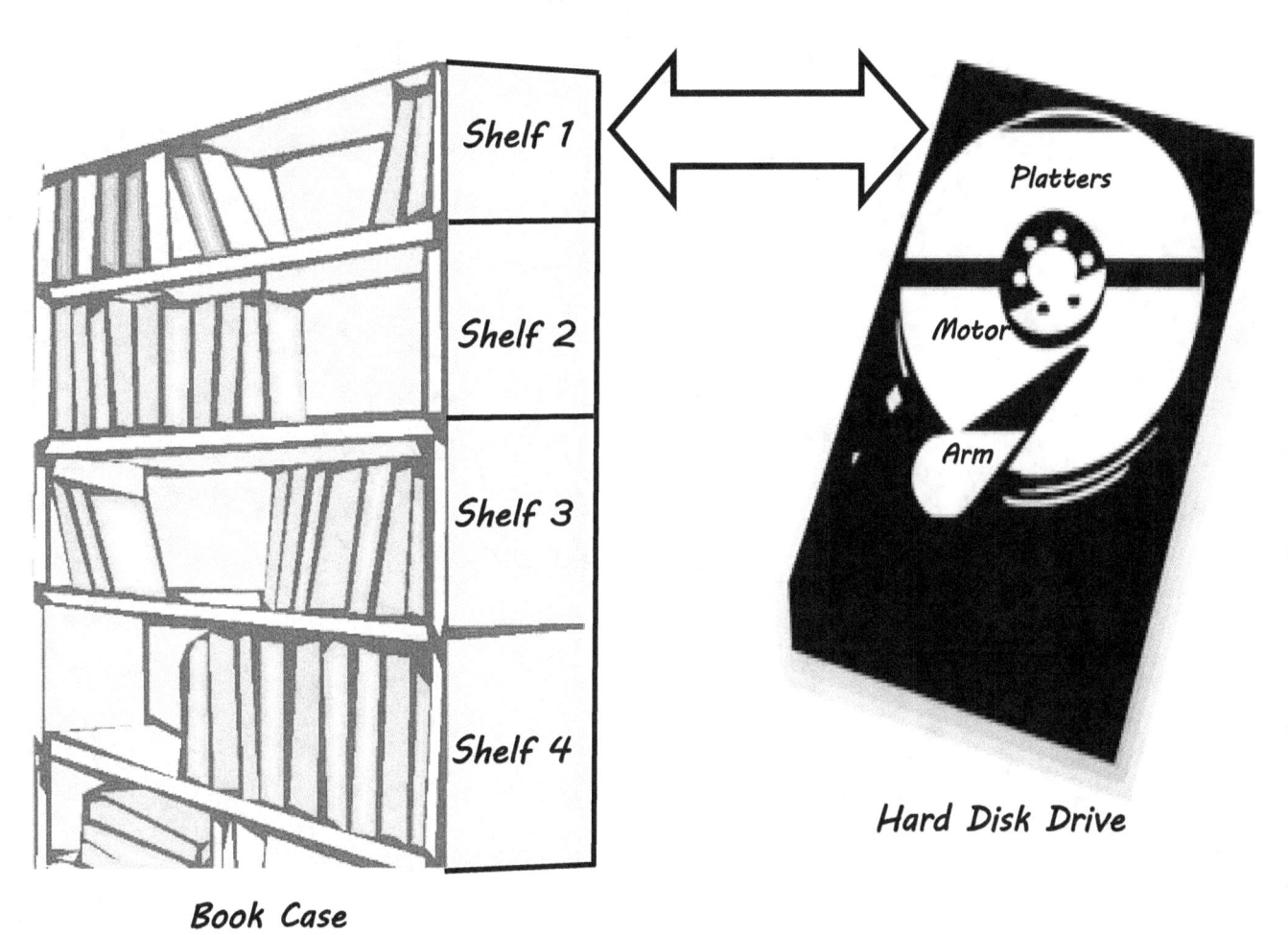

Book Case

Hard Disk Drive

Data Inside HDD or SSD

There is only one way to save data on HDD (or SSD) and that is in the form of file. File(s) you can put inside the Folder (also known as Directory). In real world, a Book Case is like a HDD (or SSD), whereas Shelves are like Folders.

Inside each shelf we have books; just like files inside a folder of HDD. Like empty book shelf in a book case, you can create a folder in HDD without a file in it which will be called as an empty folder.

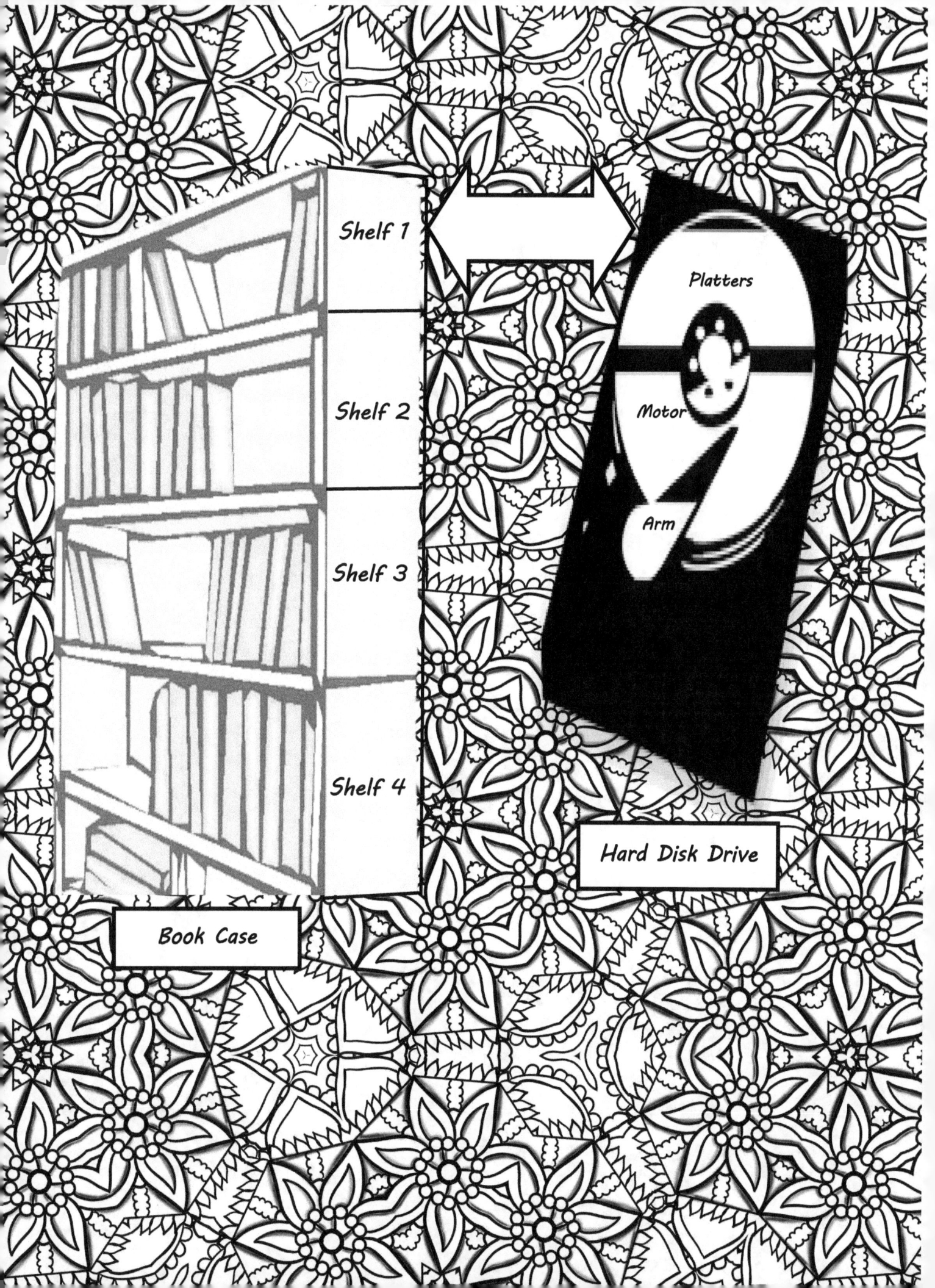

Shelf 1

Shelf 2

Shelf 3

Shelf 4

Platters

Motor

Arm

Hard Disk Drive

Book Case

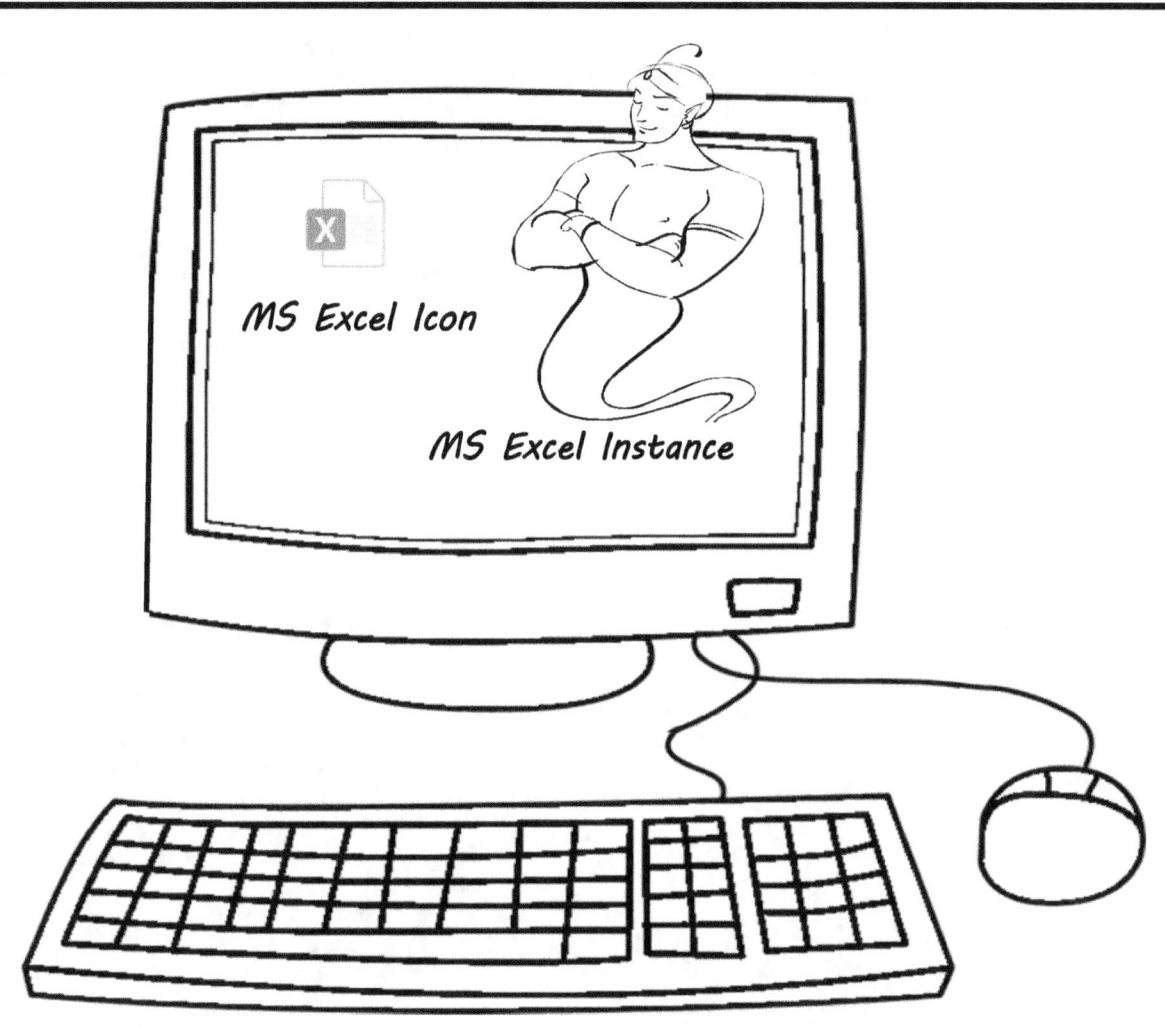

Movie ID	Movie Name	Release Date
1	Mickie Mouse	10/1/1981
2	King Kong	9/12/1991

MS Excel Instance Benefits

When we purchase MS Office Suite, it comes with MS Excel software along with MS Word, MS PowerPoint etc. The software we download is called <u>uninstalled software</u>. After installation, we run it to make instance of installed software. MS Excel instance help us save data in the form of rows (called records) and columns (called fields). The table shown above has three rows and three columns.

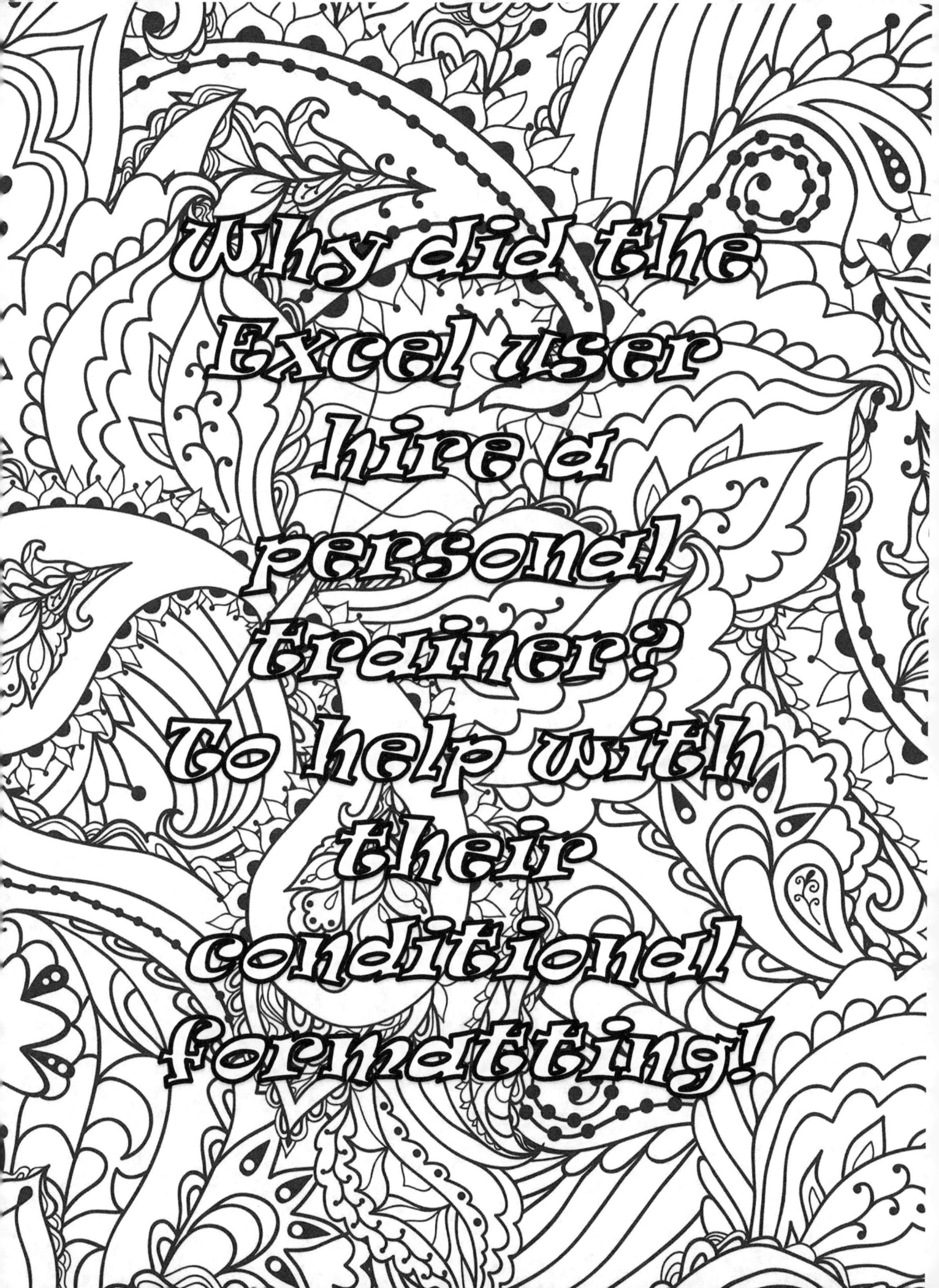

Movie ID	Movie Name	Release Date
1	Mickie Mouse	10/1/1981
2	King Kong	9/12/1991

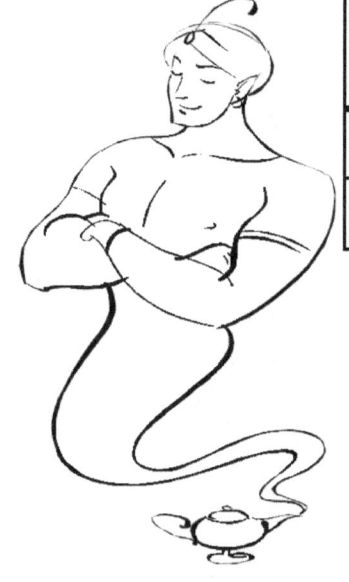

Student ID	Student Name	Grade
1001	Jane	6
1002	Tom	7

MS Excel Instance 1

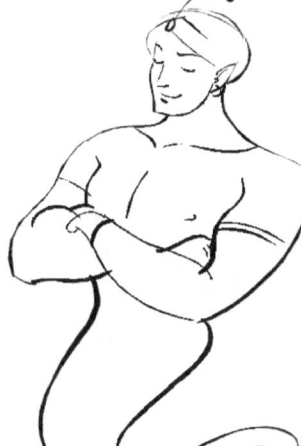

MS Excel Instance 2

MS Excel Multiple Instances

On your computer, you can launch multiple instances of MS Excel and each having a separate MS Excel file mounted on it. MS Excel file is called MS Excel Workbook. Each MS Excel workbook contains one or more MS Excel worksheets. Each worksheet has 100s of blank columns and rows.

Why did the Excel work-sheet get in a fight with the Word docu-ment?
It thought the Word document was a spread-sheet imposter!

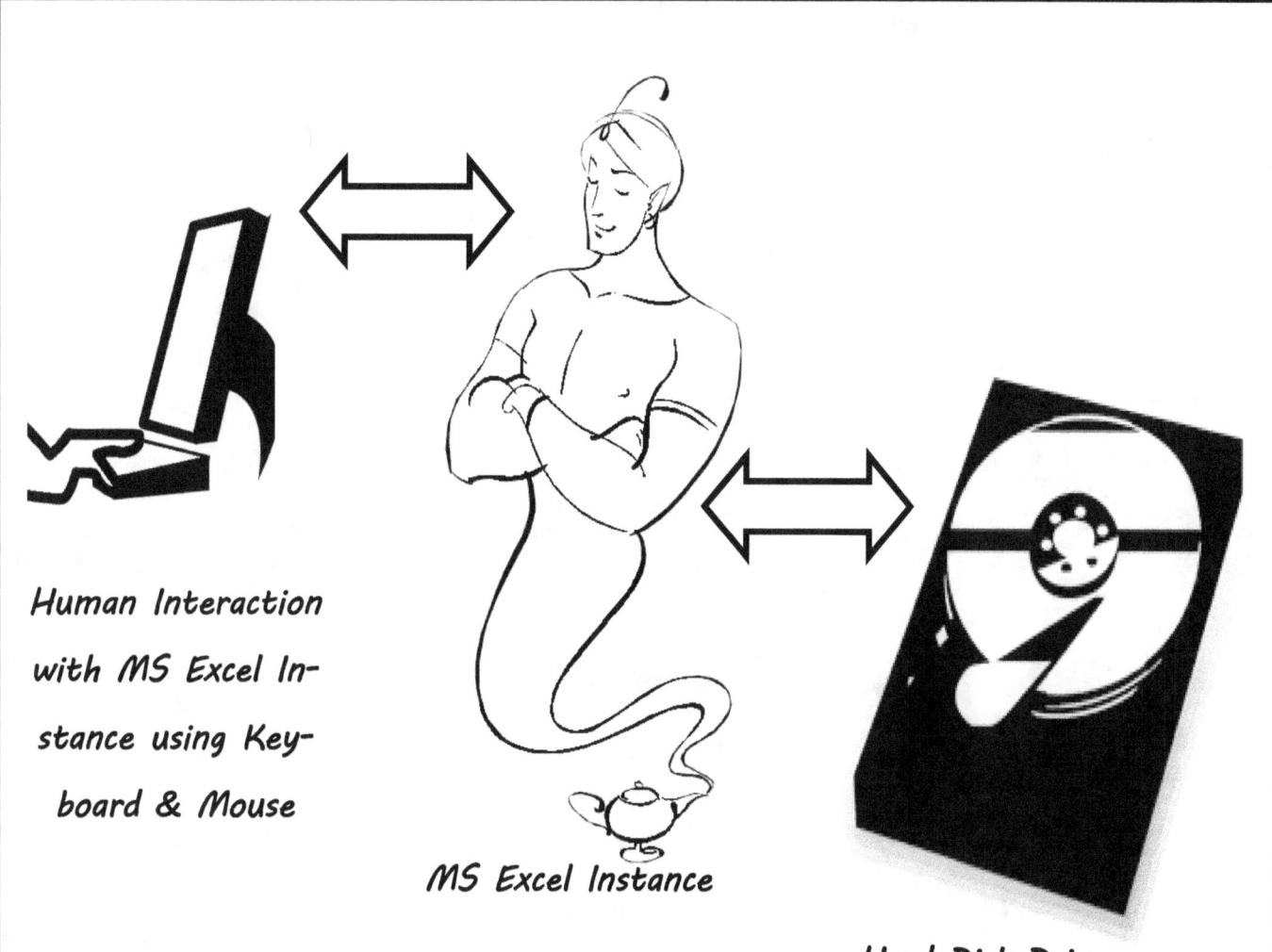

Human Interaction with MS Excel Instance using Keyboard & Mouse

MS Excel Instance

Hard Disk Drive

Movie ID	Movie Name	Release Date
1	Mickie Mouse	10/1/1981
2	King Kong	9/12/1991

MS Excel Workbooks on Hard Disk Drive

MS Excel Instance saves the data for permanent storage on Hard Disk Drive whenever we click the save button on MS Excel Instance's Graphical User Interface (GUI).

How many hard disks does it take to change a light bulb? None, they prefer the dark.

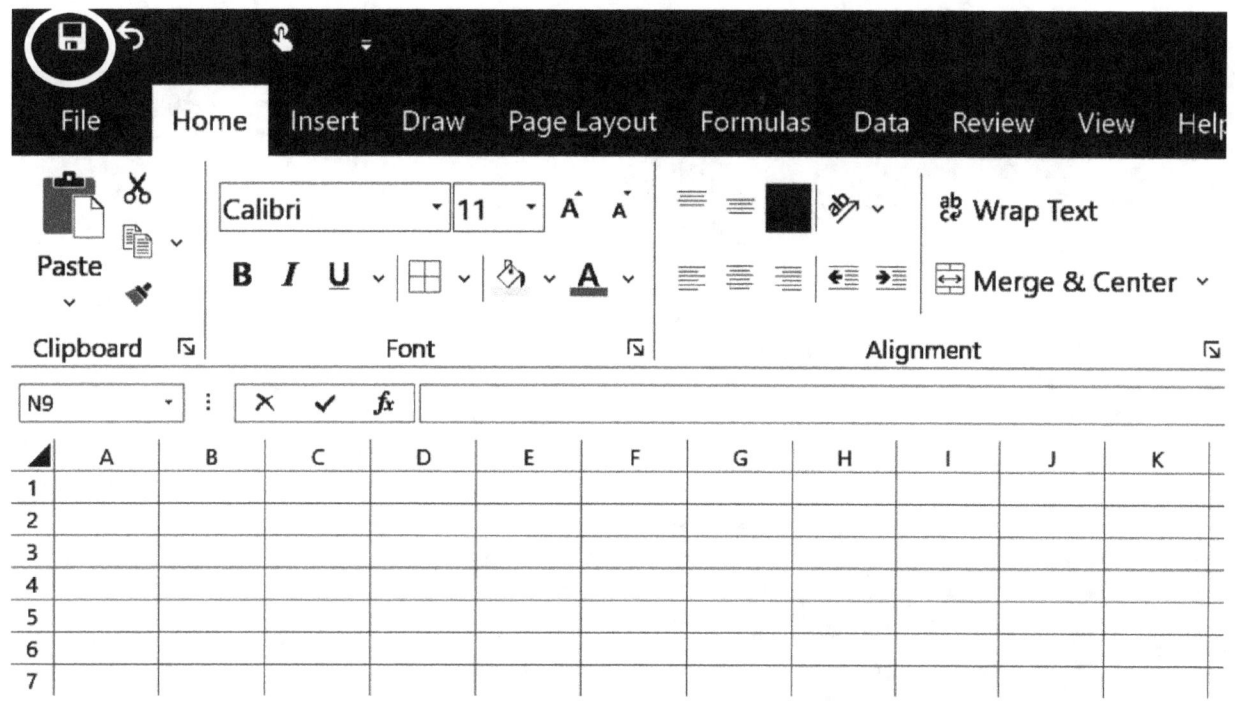

MS Excel Instance's Graphical User Interface (GUI)

Human ~ Excel Instance Interaction

Human Interaction with MS Excel Instance takes place using Keyboard & Mouse and MS Excel Instance's Graphical User Interface. When we are done populating the data in the spreadsheet then we press the save button (circled top left corner of the screenshot of MS Excel GUI) and the MS Excel Instance saves the MS Excel file on the hard disk drive.

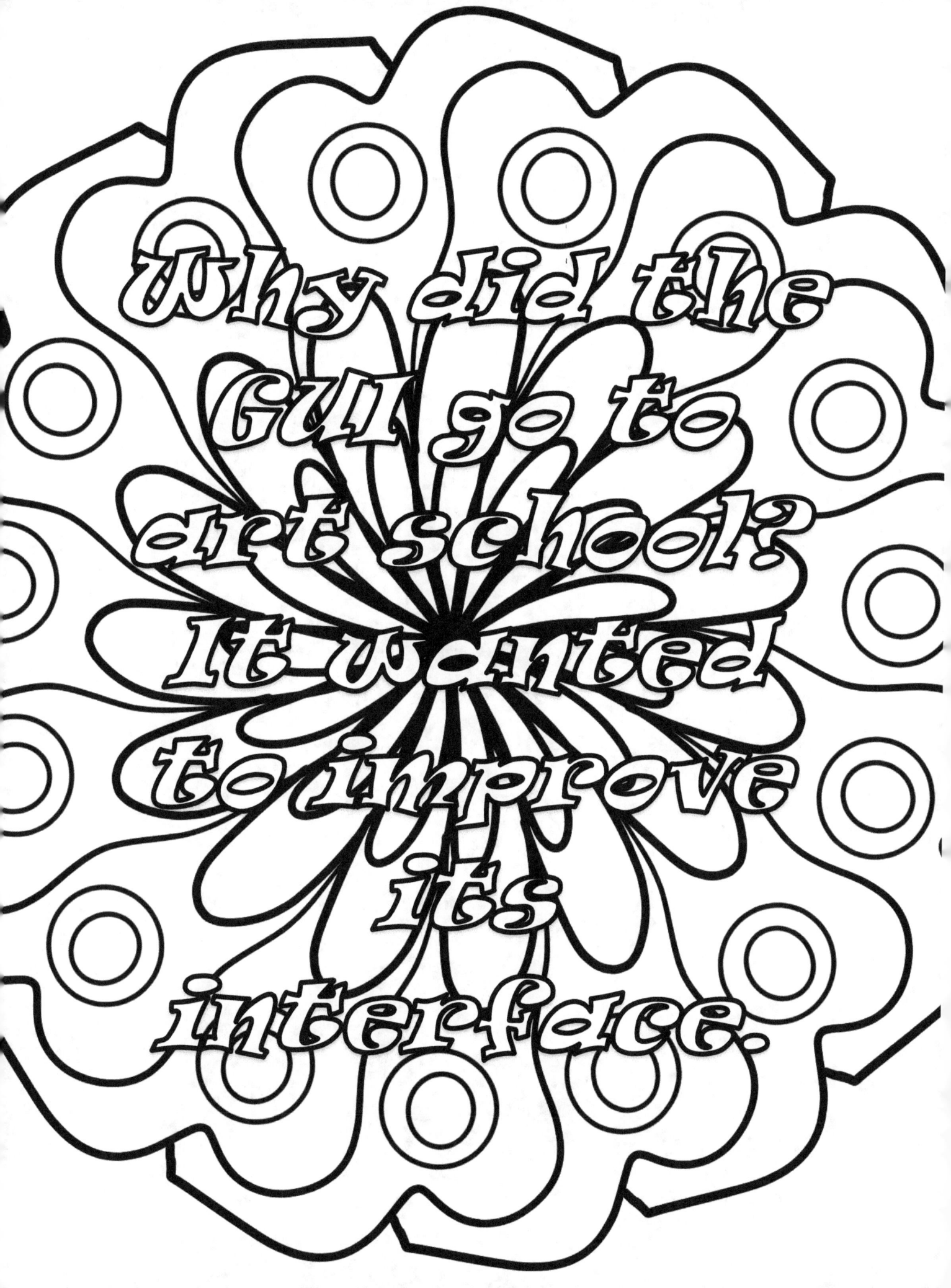

Why did the Gull go to art school? It wanted to improve its interface.

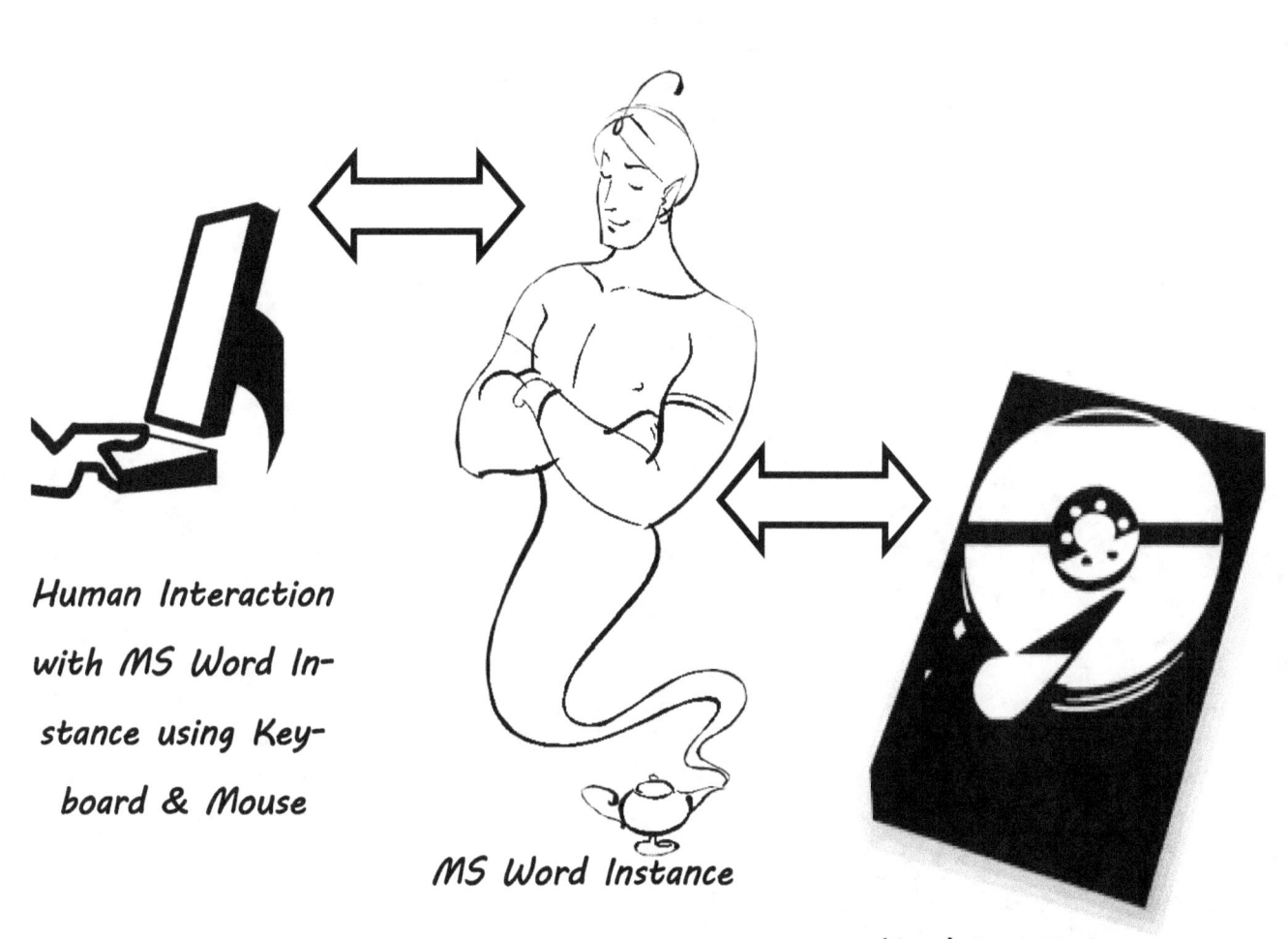

Human Interaction with MS Word Instance using Keyboard & Mouse

MS Word Instance

Hard Disk Drive

Movie ID	Movie Name	Release Date
1	Mickie Mouse	10/1/1981
2	King Kong	9/12/1991

MS Word Document File on Hard Disk Drive

MS Word Instance saves the data for permanent storage on Hard Disk Drive whenever we click the save button on MS Word Instance's _Graphical User Interface_ (GUI).

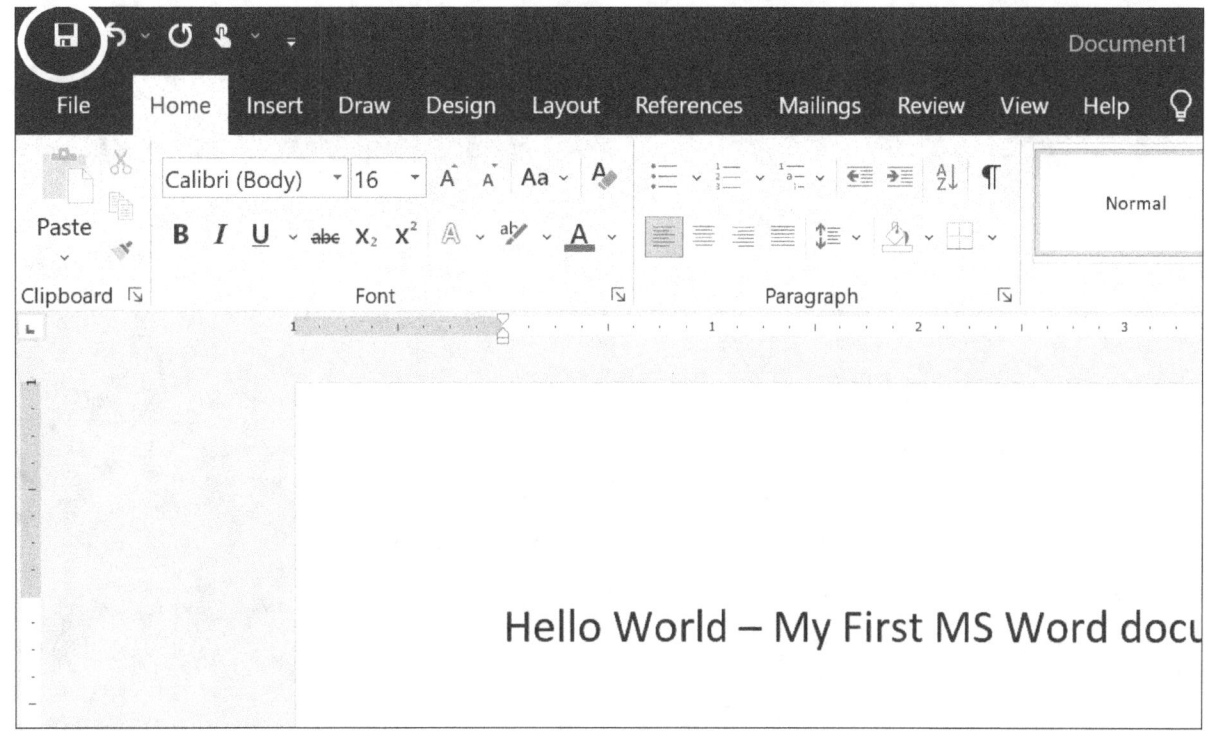

MS Word Instance's Graphical User Interface (GUI)

Human ~ MS Word Instance Interaction

Human Interaction with MS Word Instance takes place using Keyboard & Mouse and MS Word Instance's Graphical User Interface. When we are done entering the data in the document then we press the save button (circled top left corner of the screenshot of MS Word GUI) and the MS Word Instance saves the MS Word document file on the hard disk drive.